WHITBY TRAVEL GUIDE 2024

"The complete insider to exploring Whitby, North Yorkshire, England holidays, adventure, culinary delights, castle, gardens, parks, top tourist attractions and hidden gems."

RICHARD SMITH

All rights reserved. No part of this publication may be reproduced, distributed, or transmitted in any form or by any means, including photocopying, recording, or other electronic or mechanical methods, without the prior written permission of the publisher, except in the case of brief quotations embodied in critical reviews and certain other noncommercial uses permitted by copyright law.

Copyright © Richard Smith, 2024.

TABLE OF CONTENTS

Introduction 5
Planning Your Trip 15
Accommodation Options 20
Exploring Whitby 25
Dining and Nightlife 34
Outdoor Activities 41
Day Trips from Whitby 48
Sample Itineraries 58
Practical Information 67
Conclusion 71

Introduction

The wind whipped my hair across my face as I stood at the edge of Whitby's harbor, the salty spray singing in my ears. Below, fishing boats bobbed like colorful corks in a vast, churning sea. It was a scene straight out of a postcard, except for the chilling whisper of a name on the breeze: Dracula.

Yes, Whitby. The very name conjures images of gothic arches, fog-shrouded cliffs, and the king of the vampires himself. But Whitby is so much more than Bram Stoker's inspiration. It's a town that breathes history, a place where the past whispers from ancient cobbled streets and the North Sea crashes against the rugged coastline.

Remember that childhood fascination with pirates and buried treasure? Whitby was once a bustling port, launching the legendary Captain Cook on his voyages of discovery. Fancy yourself a history buff? Wander the ruins of Whitby Abbey, a testament to medieval faith, or delve into the town's maritime past at the Captain Cook Memorial Museum.

Maybe, like me, you're drawn to the darker side of things. Then Whitby offers a chilling thrill. Walk in Dracula's footsteps on a themed tour, or lose yourself in the interactive "Dracula Experience." But fear not, even the bravest vampire hunter will find solace in Whitby's welcoming pubs and award-winning seafood restaurants.

This book is your ultimate guide to unlocking the secrets of Whitby. Whether you're a history buff, a Dracula devotee, or simply a traveler seeking a unique and captivating escape, Whitby has something for you. So, pack your bags, grab this guide, and let's embark on an unforgettable adventure together!

History and Culture

Whitby, a captivating town nestled on the Yorkshire Coast, boasts a history as rich and dramatic as the North Sea that crashes against its shores. Its story unfolds like a captivating novel, with chapters dedicated to faith, exploration, industry, and a touch of the macabre.

From Monastery to Maritime Hub:

Our tale begins in the 7th century AD, when King Oswiu of Northumbria established a monastery on the windswept headland above the River Esk. This sacred site, known as Whitby Abbey, became a beacon of learning and spirituality, attracting scholars like the Abbess Hilda, whose synod in 664 AD helped shape the Christian calendar.

Centuries rolled by, and the tides of fortune shifted. Viking raids in the 9th and 10th centuries left their mark, but Whitby persevered. By the Middle Ages, the town had transformed into a thriving port, fueled by the lucrative trade in alum, a mineral used in dyeing textiles. The discovery of vast alum deposits nearby propelled Whitby onto the international stage.

The Age of Exploration and Whitby's Son:

The 18th century witnessed a momentous shift. Whitby emerged as a major shipbuilding center, its docks teeming with activity. Among the young men drawn to the town's maritime energy was a bright-eyed apprentice named James Cook. Little did anyone know that this unassuming sailor would etch his name onto the map of the world. Cook's apprenticeship in Whitby honed his skills, and his voyages of discovery aboard the Endeavour, built right here in Whitby's shipyard, would forever change our understanding of the Pacific Ocean and beyond.

A Town Forged by Industry and Innovation:

Whitby's maritime prowess extended beyond exploration. The town developed a robust whaling industry, with ships venturing to the far corners of the Arctic in pursuit of valuable whale oil. However, the brutal realities of whaling eventually led to its decline in the 19th century.

Fortunately, Whitby found new avenues for prosperity. The discovery of jet, a black gemstone formed from fossilized wood, sparked a thriving local industry. Whitby jet jewelry became a coveted fashion statement, worn by royalty and commoners alike. The town's cobbled streets echoed with the clatter of workshops, where skilled artisans crafted intricate pieces that continue to captivate modern audiences.

The Gothic Allure and Dracula's Legacy:

Whitby's allure extends beyond its maritime and industrial heritage. The town's dramatic setting, with its ruined abbey perched on windswept cliffs, captivated the imagination of Irish novelist Bram

Stoker. In 1897, Stoker visited Whitby, and the town's gothic atmosphere seeped into his mind. The result? Dracula, a chilling novel that propelled Whitby into the realm of the macabre.

Today, Whitby proudly embraces its Dracula connection. The town holds annual Dracula festivals, themed tours delve into the novel's settings, and the Dracula Experience offers a thrilling interactive adventure. Whether a fan of the book or simply drawn by the gothic atmosphere, Whitby offers a unique blend of history and literary mystique.

Geography and Climate

Whitby's dramatic geography plays a central role in its character. The town sits on a narrow strip of land between the North Sea and the River Esk, nestled within the North York Moors National Park. The coastline is a spectacle of rugged beauty, with towering cliffs carved by relentless waves. The wind whips through the streets, carrying the salty tang of the sea and the scent of seaweed.

The climate here is moderate, influenced by the North Atlantic Drift. Summers are generally mild with pleasantly warm days and cool nights.

Winters are relatively mild as well, though occasional spells of cold weather can bring frosts and occasional snow flurries.

The ever-present wind is a defining feature of Whitby's weather. It can be invigorating on a sunny day, but also quite fierce during winter storms. The sea can be equally unpredictable, with calm turquoise waters giving way to dramatic swells and crashing waves.

Despite these elements, Whitby's natural beauty is undeniable. The town offers a plethora of opportunities to experience its dramatic landscape. Hike along the Cleveland Way National Trail, which stretches along the cliffs, offering breathtaking panoramic views of the coastline. Take a boat tour to spot playful seals basking on the rocks or majestic dolphins leaping through the waves. Or simply wander along the harbor walls, soaking in the raw power of the North Sea.

Whitby's rich history, intertwined with its captivating geography and climate, creates a unique and memorable experience for visitors. It's a town where the past whispers in crumbling stone, the present hums with maritime activity, and the wind carries echoes of both exploration and gothic mystery.

Why visit Whitby

Whitby offers a unique tapestry of experiences, and here are some distinct reasons why it should be your next travel destination:

1. Unearth Whitby's Dark Secrets:

- **Dracula's Inspiration:** Step into the world of Bram Stoker's iconic novel. Whitby's gothic atmosphere and dramatic setting were the driving force behind Dracula. Take a themed tour, visit the atmospheric Dracula Experience, or simply wander the streets where Stoker himself found inspiration.

- **A Touch of the Macabre:** For those who enjoy a bit of the spooky, Whitby offers a unique blend of history and the supernatural. Explore the folklore surrounding the town, visit ancient graveyards perched on windswept cliffs, or delve into the local legends of ghosts and ghouls.

2. Journey Through Time:

- **Monastery's Echoes:** Whitby Abbey, a magnificent ruin overlooking the town, whispers tales of a bygone era. Explore the remnants of this 7th-century monastery, imagine the lives of monks and pilgrims, and learn about its role in shaping the religious landscape of England.

- **Maritime Marvels:** Immerse yourself in Whitby's rich maritime history. Visit the Captain Cook Memorial Museum and learn about the town's role in launching legendary voyages of discovery. Explore the harbor, a hub of activity since medieval times, and witness the legacy of Whitby's seafaring spirit.

3. **Embrace the Beauty of Nature:**

    - **Dramatic Coastline:** Hike along the Cleveland Way National Trail, a path that hugs the rugged cliffs offering breathtaking panoramic views of the North Sea. Witness the power of nature, feel the invigorating wind, and appreciate the ever-changing moods of the coastline.
    - **Wildlife Encounters:** Embark on a boat trip and witness the diverse marine life that thrives off the Whitby coast. Spot playful seals basking on rocks, dolphins leaping

through the waves, or even migrating whales breaching the surface in the distance.

4. **Discover a Treasure Trove:**

   - **Whitby Jet:** Unearth the unique black gemstone found only in Whitby. Visit the Whitby Jet Heritage Centre to delve into its history, from prehistoric beginnings to the Victorian mourning jewelry craze. Explore local shops and find the perfect piece of Whitby Jet jewelry, a genuine treasure to take home.

   - **Foodie Paradise:** Indulge in some of the best fish and chips in the UK. Whitby's fresh seafood caught right off the harbor boasts unparalleled taste. Explore charming cafes, traditional tea rooms, and local pubs for a variety of culinary delights.

5. **Immerse Yourself in Culture:**

   - **Festival Fun:** Whitby comes alive with vibrant festivals throughout the year. Immerse yourself in the Whitby Goth Weekend, a celebration of goth culture, or partake in other festivities that showcase the town's unique character.

- **Art and Architecture:** Explore the Pannett Art Gallery, showcasing local and national artwork. Admire the architectural details of historic buildings like the Church of St Mary and the Whitby Spa Pavilion, a Victorian masterpiece overlooking the sea.

Planning Your Trip

Whitby beckons with its dramatic coastline, rich history, and a touch of the gothic. To ensure a smooth and enjoyable journey, here's a comprehensive guide to planning your Whitby escape.

When to Visit:

Whitby's charm unfolds throughout the year, each season offering a unique perspective. Here's a breakdown to help you choose the perfect time:

- **Spring (March-May):** Spring awakens Whitby from its winter slumber. The crowds are smaller, wildflowers paint the landscape in vibrant hues, and the sea retains a winter chill, perfect for brisk walks along the coast. This is a good time for budget-conscious travelers to find deals on accommodation.

- **Summer (June-August):** Summer brings longer days, warm sunshine, and a vibrant atmosphere. The town bustles with tourists, festivals like the Whitby Regatta liven up the harbor, and boat trips offer ample opportunities for wildlife spotting. Be prepared for higher accommodation prices and larger crowds during peak season.

- **Autumn (September-November):** Autumn paints Whitby in stunning colors. The crowds begin to thin, the temperatures remain pleasant, and the sea takes on a dramatic, stormy character. This is a fantastic time for photographers to capture the town's beauty under a constantly changing sky.

- **Winter (December-February):** Winter transforms Whitby into a wonderland. The town twinkles with festive lights, cozy pubs offer a warm refuge from the elements, and the possibility of seeing the Northern Lights adds a touch of magic. Be aware that some shops and restaurants may have reduced hours during this season.

Getting There:

By Air: The nearest major airport is Manchester Airport (MAN), located approximately 1.5 hours away by car or train. From Manchester Airport, take a train directly to Whitby or connect through Middlesbrough station. Alternatively, Leeds

Bradford Airport (LBA) is another option, though with slightly less frequent connections to Whitby.

By Train: Whitby is well-connected to major cities in the UK by train. Direct trains run from Manchester Piccadilly and York, offering a comfortable and scenic journey. For those coming from further afield, connecting trains are readily available.

By Car: Whitby is easily accessible by car. From the south, take the A1(M) northbound and follow signs for the A64 towards Scarborough and Whitby. From the north, take the A19 southbound and follow signs for Whitby. Be aware that parking in Whitby can be challenging, especially during peak season. Consider car parks outside the town center and walk or take a taxi to your accommodation.

Getting Around Whitby:

Walking: The best way to experience Whitby's charming streets and historic harbor is on foot. Most of the town center is easily walkable, allowing you to soak in the atmosphere and hidden gems at your own pace.

Bus: Whitby has a local bus service that connects the town center with surrounding areas. This is a convenient option for exploring nearby villages like Robin Hood's Bay or Sandsend.

Taxis: Taxis are readily available in Whitby, particularly at the train station and harbor. This is a convenient option for getting back to your accommodation after a night out or for those with limited mobility.

Bicycle: If you're feeling adventurous, consider renting a bicycle. The surrounding countryside offers a network of scenic cycling paths, perfect for exploring the North York Moors National Park. Be aware of traffic regulations and ensure you are comfortable cycling on hilly terrain.

Visa and Entry Requirements:

For Citizens of the United States, Canada, Australia, and New Zealand: citizens of these countries do not require a visa for visits to the UK of up to 6 months. However, you will need to obtain an Electronic Travel Authorization (ETA) prior to your departure. This is a quick and straightforward online process.

For Citizens of Other Countries:

Visa requirements can vary depending on your nationality. We recommend checking the official UK government website for the latest information on visa requirements and entry procedures: https://www.gov.uk/check-uk-visa

Additional Tips:

- **Currency:** The United Kingdom uses the British Pound Sterling (GBP). Consider exchanging currency before your trip or using an ATM upon arrival.

- **Language:** English is the primary language spoken in Whitby.

- **Travel Insurance:** It's highly recommended to purchase travel insurance before your trip to cover any unforeseen circumstances.

- **Packing:** Whitby's weather can be unpredictable. Pack layers of clothing that can be easily adjusted to suit the changing conditions. Don't forget comfortable walking shoes for exploring the town and waterproof gear for potential rain showers.

Accommodation Options

Whitby offers a diverse range of accommodation options to suit every budget and travel style. Whether you crave a luxurious stay overlooking the harbor, a charming B&B with a local feel, or a self-catering cottage for a family getaway, Whitby has you covered. Here's a glimpse into the accommodation options awaiting you:

Luxury on the Waterfront:

Indulge in unparalleled comfort and breathtaking views with a stay in one of Whitby's luxury hotels. These establishments boast prime locations on the waterfront, offering stunning vistas of the harbor and easy access to the town's attractions. Expect spacious rooms with plush furnishings, top-notch amenities like spas and fitness centers, and impeccable service. Savor delectable meals at on-site restaurants with seasonal menus featuring fresh, local seafood.

Charming Boutique Hotels:

For a touch of personalized charm, consider a boutique hotel. These smaller, characterful establishments often occupy historic buildings, some dating back centuries. Expect unique decor, intimate settings, and a focus on personalized service. Boutique hotels often partner with local businesses, offering guests exclusive discounts or experiences.

Traditional Bed and Breakfasts (B&Bs):

Immerse yourself in the warmth and hospitality of a traditional B&B. Many Whitby B&Bs are family-run establishments housed in charming Victorian townhouses. Expect comfortable rooms, a hearty breakfast prepared with local ingredients, and the opportunity to interact with friendly hosts who can offer insider tips on exploring the town.

Cosy Self-Catering Cottages:

For a home away from home experience, consider a self-catering cottage. Whitby offers a wide range of cottages to choose from, ranging from quaint studios perfect for couples to spacious houses ideal for families or groups. Self-catering cottages offer the flexibility to prepare your own meals and enjoy the freedom of having your own space. Many cottages boast charming features like fireplaces, private gardens, and stunning sea views.

Unique Whitby Stays:

For the adventurous traveler, Whitby offers some truly unique accommodation options. Consider glamping in a luxury pod nestled amidst the North York Moors National Park, offering a blend of rustic charm with modern amenities. Alternatively, book a stay in a converted boathouse on the harbor, where you can wake up to the gentle rocking of the waves and panoramic sea views.

Considerations When Choosing Your Accommodation:

- **Location:** Do you want to be in the heart of the action on the waterfront, or prefer a quieter location near the beach?

- **Budget:** Luxury hotels offer top-notch amenities, but come at a premium price. B&Bs and self-catering cottages provide a more budget-friendly option.

- **Travel Style:** Are you looking for a social hub with a bar and restaurant, or a cozy retreat for relaxation?

- **Travel Party:** Consider the size of your group when choosing accommodation. B&Bs and hotels cater well to couples and solo travelers, while cottages offer flexibility for families or larger groups.

Exploring Whitby

Whitby unfolds like a captivating storybook, each chapter revealing a unique landmark waiting to be explored. Here's your guide to some of the town's most enchanting destinations:

Whitby Abbey:

Towering over Whitby like a sentinel from the past, Whitby Abbey whispers tales of faith, power, and resilience. Founded in the 7th century AD by King Oswiu of Northumbria, the abbey became a beacon of learning and spirituality, attracting scholars like the Abbess Hilda. Explore the dramatic ruins, marveling at the intricate stonework and remnants of the cloisters, refectory, and church. Imagine the monks chanting in the halls and the pilgrims who once walked these grounds. Climb the 199 Steps for breathtaking panoramic views of the town, harbor, and the vast expanse of the North Sea. Whitby Abbey also hosts regular events and exhibitions, bringing the past to life for visitors.

Whitby Harbour:

The beating heart of Whitby, the harbour pulsates with a timeless energy. Cobbled streets lead down to the water's edge, where colorful fishing boats bob gently in the waves. Inhale the salty sea air as you watch fishermen unload their daily catch, a testament to Whitby's enduring maritime heritage. Take a leisurely stroll along the harbor walls, soaking in the vibrant atmosphere. Explore the quirky shops selling nautical souvenirs, fresh seafood stalls, and traditional pubs offering a taste of local life. Consider a boat trip for a chance to spot playful seals basking on rocks, majestic dolphins leaping through the waves, or even whales breaching on the horizon. Experience the thrill of a sunset cruise, where the golden light paints the harbor with a magical glow.

Captain Cook Memorial Museum

Step into the world of James Cook, Whitby's most famous son. The Captain Cook Memorial Museum is housed in the very building where Cook lodged as an apprentice shipbuilder. Explore exhibits that delve into his pioneering voyages across the Pacific Ocean, the South Atlantic, and the Arctic. See meticulously crafted models of Cook's ships, pore over handwritten logs and maps, and marvel at the navigational instruments that guided him on his epic journeys. Learn about the impact Cook's discoveries had on the world, expanding our understanding of geography, trade, and indigenous cultures. The museum offers a fascinating glimpse into the life and legacy of this legendary explorer.

St. Mary's Church:

Standing tall on the East Cliff, St. Mary's Church offers a glimpse into Whitby's rich religious history. Built in the 12th century, the church boasts stunning gothic architecture, with soaring arches, stained glass windows that tell biblical stories, and elaborate stonework. Climb the tower for panoramic views of the town and harbor, and explore the fascinating graveyard, where weathered headstones whisper tales of Whitby's past residents. St. Mary's Church serves as a place of peace and reflection, a reminder of the enduring power of faith in this historic town.

Whitby Museum:

Delve into the social and cultural tapestry of Whitby at the Whitby Museum. Housed in a grand Victorian building within Pannett Park, the museum's displays showcase the town's evolution

30

from a thriving monastic center to a bustling maritime hub. Learn about Whitby's whaling industry, a once-lucrative trade that shaped the town's economic and social landscape. Discover the art of Whitby jet, a unique black gemstone found only in the area, and explore a timeline of the town's development. Temporary exhibitions often bring fresh perspectives to Whitby's rich history, ensuring a dynamic museum experience for every visitor.

Pannett Park:

Escape the hustle and bustle of the town center at Pannett Park. This sprawling green space offers a haven for relaxation and recreation. Stroll along manicured lawns, admire the vibrant floral displays, and take a moment to breathe in the fresh air. Children will delight in the playground equipment, while a miniature railway provides a fun and scenic ride for all ages. Pannett Park also hosts open-air concerts and festivals throughout the year, adding to the vibrant atmosphere.

Whitby Beach:

Unwind and embrace the beauty of the North Sea at Whitby Beach. This vast stretch of golden sand stretches for two miles, offering ample space for sunbathing, playing beach games, or simply soaking up the coastal atmosphere. Take a refreshing dip in the cool waters, or build sandcastles with the whole family. Explore the colorful beach huts, a quintessential feature of the British seaside, and find the perfect spot to relax and enjoy the stunning sea views. During the summer months, you'll find ice cream vendors, donkey rides, and traditional seaside entertainment adding to the festive beach atmosphere. At low tide, explore the rock pools teeming with marine life, a natural wonder that sparks curiosity in children and adults alike. As the sun dips below the horizon, Whitby Beach transforms into a spectacular setting for watching the sunset paint the sky in vibrant hues.

Dining and Nightlife

Whitby tantalizes not only with its history and beauty, but also with its diverse culinary scene and lively nightlife. From traditional pub fare to award-winning restaurants, Whitby caters to every taste bud and social preference. Let's embark on a delicious and entertaining exploration of Whitby's dining and nightlife offerings.

A Taste of Tradition:

plate of golden fish and chips with mushy peas and a wedge of lemon on a white paper plate

Whitby's culinary heritage is deeply rooted in its maritime history. Fresh seafood reigns supreme, with "fish and chips" taking center stage. Whitby's fish and chips are legendary, boasting the freshest catches hauled straight from the North Sea. Crispy battered fish, flaky and succulent, paired with golden chips (French fries for our American readers) and mushy peas makes for a simple yet incredibly satisfying meal. For a local twist, try the "skappi" - a traditional dish of boiled bread soaked in a rich fish broth.

Beyond Fish and Chips:

While fish and chips are a must-try, Whitby offers a delightful spectrum of culinary options. Indulge in a hearty seafood stew, a comforting combination of fresh fish, shellfish, and vegetables simmered in a flavorful broth. Sample local kippers, herring that have been smoked over oak chips, for a unique and smoky flavor. Venture beyond the sea with traditional Yorkshire dishes like "toad in the hole" (sausages baked in a Yorkshire pudding batter) or a comforting "bangers and mash" (sausages and mashed potatoes).

Best Restaurants and Cafes:

Fine Dining:

- **The Star Inn The Harbour:** Boasting breathtaking views of the harbor, The Star Inn The Harbour offers an upscale dining experience. Their menu features the freshest local seafood, expertly prepared and beautifully presented. Indulge in lobster thermidor, pan-seared scallops, or a succulent steak while soaking in the captivating harbor panorama.

- **The Magpie Café:** For a taste of Whitby's culinary heritage with a modern twist, head to The Magpie Café. This award-winning establishment focuses on sustainable seafood, offering innovative dishes that showcase the bounty of the North Sea. Their signature Magpie pie, a flaky pastry filled with a rich seafood stew, is a must-try.

Casual Dining:

- **Harry's Lounge Bar & Brasserie:** Harry's offers a relaxed yet stylish setting for enjoying modern British cuisine. Their menu features fresh, seasonal ingredients, with vegetarian and gluten-free options available. Savor classic dishes like fish and chips with a gourmet touch, or indulge in a juicy steak burger with homemade fries.

- **The Shoreline Restaurant:** Located right on the seafront, The Shoreline

Restaurant offers stunning views alongside delicious food. Their menu caters to all tastes, with seafood dishes, pasta specialties, and vegetarian options. Enjoy a leisurely lunch on the terrace, watching the boats bob in the harbor.

Cafes:

- **Madocks Cafe:** For a quintessential English tea room experience, look no further than Madocks Cafe. This charming cafe boasts a delightful selection of homemade cakes and pastries, perfect for a sweet treat or a light afternoon tea. Choose from a variety of loose-leaf teas and freshly brewed coffee to complement your sweet indulgence.

- **The Harbour View Cafe:** Located on the West Cliff, The Harbour View Cafe offers stunning panoramic views of the harbor and coastline. This cozy cafe is a great spot to grab a coffee and a breakfast sandwich while enjoying the fresh sea air and breathtaking scenery.

Pubs and Bars: Unveiling Whitby's Lively Side

No exploration of Whitby's nightlife is complete without experiencing the charm of its traditional pubs. Step into a warm and welcoming pub, adorned with wooden beams and brass fittings, and soak in the friendly atmosphere. Sample a selection of local ales and ciders, brewed in the region with unique flavors. Many pubs also offer live music nights or pub quizzes, providing a fun and social environment.

For the Beer Enthusiast:

- **The Whitby Brewery:** Immerse yourself in Whitby's brewing heritage at The Whitby Brewery. This award-winning brewery offers tours and tastings, allowing you to sample their diverse selection of ales, lagers, and seasonal brews. Pair your beer with a delicious pub meal in their on-site restaurant.
- **The Old Ferryman:** Dating back to the 18th century, The Old Ferryman is a historic pub steeped in atmosphere. Enjoy a pint of real ale next to a crackling fireplace, or soak up the sunshine in their beer garden

overlooking the harbor. They also host regular live music nights featuring local musicians.

For the Cocktail Connoisseur:

- **The Waiting Room:** This stylish bar offers a sophisticated setting for enjoying expertly crafted cocktails. Their menu features classic cocktails with a twist, alongside innovative creations using seasonal ingredients. The Waiting Room also boasts an extensive selection of gins, perfect for those who appreciate this botanical spirit.

For a Lively Atmosphere:

- **The Duke of York:** Located right on the harbor, The Duke of York is a popular spot for enjoying a drink with stunning views. This lively pub attracts both locals and tourists, creating a vibrant atmosphere. They often have live music or DJ nights, making it a great place to dance the night away.

- **The Buck Inn:** A traditional pub with a modern twist, The Buck Inn caters to a younger crowd. They offer a wide selection of beers, wines, and spirits, as well as a menu of pub classics and bar snacks. Their large screen TVs show sporting events, and they often host themed nights, making it a fun and social spot.

Whitby's nightlife caters to every mood. Whether you seek a cozy pub with a crackling fireplace and a pint of local ale, a stylish bar with innovative cocktails, or a lively venue with music and dancing, Whitby has something special waiting for you.

Outdoor Activities

Whitby isn't just about history and charm; it's a playground for outdoor enthusiasts. From breathtaking coastal walks to exhilarating water sports, Whitby offers a plethora of activities to get your heart racing and immerse yourself in the beauty of the North York Moors National Park. Lace up your walking boots, grab your swimsuit, or dust off your clubs, and prepare to experience the best of Whitby's outdoor offerings.

Walking and Hiking Trails:

Whitby is a walker's paradise, with a network of trails catering to all levels of experience. Embrace the dramatic beauty of the coastline on the Cleveland Way National Trail, a 109-mile path that hugs the cliffs . As you traverse this iconic trail, you'll be rewarded with breathtaking panoramas of the North Sea, dramatic cliff formations, and charming coastal villages.

For a shorter but equally rewarding option, explore the cliff-top trails between Whitby and Robin Hood's Bay, a charming fishing village with a unique history. The trail weaves through rolling fields, offering glimpses of the glistening sea and the imposing ruins of Whitby Abbey. Robin Hood's Bay itself is a delight to explore, with its narrow cobbled streets, picturesque cottages, and a vibrant harbor.

Venture inland and explore the rolling hills and hidden valleys of the North York Moors National Park. Several established trails meander through this stunning landscape, leading you past enchanting waterfalls, ancient stone circles, and quaint villages. Whether you're seeking a challenging multi-day trek or a leisurely afternoon stroll, the North York Moors National Park offers an abundance of trails to suit your pace and interests.

Whitby Whale Watching:

Embark on an unforgettable adventure and witness the awe-inspiring spectacle of whales breaching the surface. Whitby's location on the North Sea makes it a prime spot for whale watching, with pods of dolphins, porpoises, minke whales, and even the occasional humpback whale gracing these waters. Several boat tour operators offer whale watching trips, led by experienced marine biologists who can share their knowledge and ensure a responsible and ethical experience. As you sail along the coastline, keep your eyes peeled for these magnificent creatures, their playful antics and breaching jumps leaving you breathless.

Fishing Trips:

For those who enjoy the thrill of the catch, Whitby offers a fantastic array of fishing trips. Charter a boat with a local skipper and head out to deeper waters in search of cod, mackerel, pollock, and even the occasional sea bass. These experienced guides will share their knowledge of the best fishing spots and techniques, ensuring a successful and enjoyable day on the water. Whether you're a seasoned angler or a curious beginner, a fishing trip in Whitby is a fantastic way to connect with nature and experience the bounty of the North Sea. Don't forget to inquire about regulations and licenses required for fishing in the area.

Surfing and Water Sports:

Whitby's dramatic coastline offers thrilling opportunities for surfers of all levels. Experienced surfers can tackle the challenging waves at Sandsend Beach, a short drive from Whitby. The powerful swells and consistent winds make this a popular spot for seasoned surfers seeking an adrenaline rush.

Beginners can take lessons and learn the basics at Saltburn-by-the-Sea, another coastal town located a short distance away. Reputable surf schools offer beginner-friendly lessons, providing all the necessary equipment and expert guidance to get you riding the waves in no time.

For those seeking a different kind of water adventure, try stand-up paddleboarding (SUP) or kayaking. Explore hidden coves and secluded beaches, navigate along the coastline, and enjoy a unique perspective of Whitby from the water. These activities are perfect for all levels and offer a relaxing way to enjoy the beauty of the North Sea.

Golfing:

Whitby is a haven for golfers, offering two exceptional courses to challenge and inspire players of all abilities. The Royal Whitby Golf Club, founded in 1883, boasts a championship course with breathtaking views of the North Sea. This challenging links course demands strategic thinking and precise shot-making, while rewarding players with stunning panoramas of the coastline. Imagine teeing off on the 18th hole, with the iconic Whitby Abbey standing sentinel in the distance and the waves crashing against the rugged cliffs below. For a truly unforgettable golfing experience, the Royal Whitby Golf Club is a must-play.

A Championship Links Course with Unparalleled Views:

Royal Whitby Golf Club is a golfer's dream, consistently ranked among the best courses in England. This traditional links course features rolling fairways dotted with gorse and heather, challenging bunkers strategically placed, and fast-drying greens that reward accuracy. The ever-present North Sea breeze adds another layer of difficulty, demanding precise shot control and strategic club selection.

Beyond the 18th Hole:

Beyond the championship course, the Royal Whitby Golf Club offers a variety of facilities to enhance your golfing experience. Practice your swing on the driving range, perfect your putting on the dedicated green, or take a lesson from one of the club's PGA-qualified professionals. After your round, relax and unwind in the clubhouse, enjoying panoramic sea views and a selection of refreshments. The clubhouse also boasts a restaurant offering delicious meals, perfect for refueling after a challenging round.

Whitby Castle Park Golf Course:

For a more relaxed golfing experience, consider Whitby Castle Park Golf Course. This charming 9-hole course offers a scenic setting nestled within the grounds of Whitby Castle. While not as challenging as the Royal Whitby Golf Club, it provides a delightful alternative for golfers seeking a leisurely round with picturesque views. Enjoy a friendly game with friends or family, followed by refreshments in the clubhouse overlooking the course.

Day Trips from Whitby

Whitby may be captivating, but its charm extends beyond its own borders. The surrounding region offers a tapestry of historical villages, dramatic landscapes, and charming coastal towns, all perfect for enriching day trips. Unpack your sense of adventure and prepare to explore these hidden gems, each offering a unique experience.

Robin Hood's Bay

Just a short drive from Whitby lies Robin Hood's Bay, a charming fishing village nestled between dramatic cliffs. This picturesque haven boasts narrow cobbled streets lined with colorful cottages, many dating back to the 18th century. Explore the maze-like alleyways, discovering hidden courtyards and quaint shops selling local crafts and souvenirs.

A Walk Through Time:

Robin Hood's Bay's history is as captivating as its scenery. The village played a vital role in the smuggling trade during the 18th and 19th centuries, with its labyrinthine streets providing ideal hiding spots for contraband. Visit the Robin Hood's Bay Museum to delve deeper into the village's fascinating past and explore a collection of artifacts depicting its smuggling heritage.

A Seaside Paradise:

Descend the steep steps leading down to the beach and discover a haven for beachcombers and nature enthusiasts. The pebble beach stretches for miles, offering a perfect spot for a leisurely stroll, fossil hunting, or simply soaking up the sunshine. For the adventurous, kayaking and stand-up paddleboarding are fantastic ways to explore the dramatic coastline from a different perspective. Afterward, grab a delicious meal of freshly caught seafood at one of the many harbourside restaurants, savoring the bounty of the North Sea.

Scarborough

Venture further south and discover Scarborough, a vibrant seaside resort boasting a rich history and lively atmosphere. Stroll along the expansive South Bay Beach, lined with colorful beach huts and a bustling promenade. For a touch of nostalgia, ride the traditional donkey carts or take a nostalgic trip on the scenic Scarborough Spa Cliff Lift, offering panoramic views of the coastline.

A Step Back in Time:

Delve into Scarborough's fascinating past by exploring its historic sites. Climb the winding path to Scarborough Castle, a formidable 12th-century fortress perched atop a cliff, offering breathtaking views of the town and harbor. Alternatively, visit the Scarborough Spa, a Victorian-era complex boasting a magnificent concert hall, a colonnade lined with shops and cafes, and a delightful sunken garden.

Family Fun:

Scarborough caters to all ages. Experience thrills and spills at Alpamare, a water park with exhilarating slides and pools. For a dose of culture, visit the Scarborough Art Gallery, showcasing a diverse collection of paintings and sculptures. Scarborough offers a delightful blend of history, seaside fun, and family-friendly activities, making it a perfect day trip destination.

North York Moors National Park

Escape the hustle and bustle of the coast and immerse yourself in the tranquility of the North York Moors National Park. This vast expanse of rolling hills, heather moorland, and picturesque villages offers a haven for nature lovers and outdoor enthusiasts. Explore the network of hiking trails, encountering cascading waterfalls, ancient stone circles, and dramatic moorland landscapes.

A Breath of Fresh Air:

One of the highlights of the North York Moors National Park is the North York Moors Railway, a heritage railway offering scenic journeys through breathtaking countryside. Climb aboard a vintage steam train and travel through charming villages, across majestic viaducts, and past idyllic countryside scenery.

Unwind and Explore:

For a more relaxed experience, visit one of the charming villages nestled within the park. Goathland, Haworth (home of the Brontë sisters), and Lastingham are just a few of these delightful villages, offering a glimpse into traditional Yorkshire life. Enjoy a quintessential afternoon tea in a cozy tearoom, explore local craft shops, or simply relax in a pub garden, soaking up the beautiful surroundings. The North York Moors National Park offers a refreshing escape from the urban environment and a chance to reconnect with nature.

Goathland (Heartbeat Country)

For fans of the British television series "Heartbeat," a visit to Goathland is a must. This charming village served as the fictional village of Aidensfield in the show. Step back in time and explore the filming locations, from the iconic Aidensfield Arms pub (the Goathland Hotel in real life) to the charming shops and cafes lining the main street. Imagine yourself transported into the 1960s world of "Heartbeat," encountering characters like PC David Stockwell and Nurse

Catherine Bellamy as you wander through the village.

Beyond the Screen:

Goathland's charm extends beyond its television fame. This delightful village boasts a rich history, with evidence of settlements dating back to the Bronze Age. Visit the St. Mary's Parish Church, a beautiful example of Norman architecture, or explore the Green Dragon pub, a traditional watering hole dating back to the 18th century.

A Picturesque Setting:

Goathland is nestled within the North York Moors National Park, offering stunning scenery right on its doorstep. Embark on a hike through the surrounding hills, enjoying breathtaking views of the rolling countryside. For a unique perspective, take a ride on the North York Moors Railway, which passes through the heart of the village. Goathland offers a delightful blend of television history, traditional charm, and stunning natural beauty.

Staithes

Venture further north and discover Staithes, a hidden gem nestled amongst dramatic cliffs on the Yorkshire Coast. This picturesque village boasts a maze of narrow lanes lined with colorful fishermen's cottages, many dating back to the 18th and 19th centuries. Explore the charming harbor, a haven for working fishing boats, and soak up the authentic atmosphere of this traditional seaside village.

A Celebration of Art:

Staithes has a rich artistic heritage, having long attracted artists inspired by its dramatic scenery and quaint charm. Visit the Captain Cook Memorial Museum & Art Gallery, housed in the former home of explorer Captain James Cook, and explore a collection of artworks depicting the village and its surroundings. Several galleries showcase the works of local artists, offering a glimpse into the vibrant artistic community of Staithes.

A Coastal Paradise:

Staithes offers a haven for nature lovers and outdoor enthusiasts. Descend the steep steps leading down to the beach and explore the dramatic coastline. Rock pools teeming with marine life await curious explorers, while the sandy beach is perfect for a leisurely stroll or a picnic lunch. For the adventurous, kayaking and stand-up paddleboarding are fantastic ways to explore the coastline from a different perspective.

Sample Itineraries

Whitby's diverse offerings cater to a variety of interests and travel styles. Whether you have a single day to explore or a weekend to delve deeper, here are some sample itineraries to inspire your Whitby adventure:

One Day in Whitby: Exploring the Highlights

Morning:

- **9:00 AM:** Start your day with a hearty breakfast at a charming cafe overlooking the harbor. Sample a traditional English breakfast or indulge in fresh pastries and coffee.
- **10:00 AM:** Embark on a journey through time by exploring the imposing ruins of Whitby Abbey. Climb the 199 Steps for breathtaking panoramic views of the town and harbor. Immerse yourself in the abbey's rich history, learning about its role as a monastery and its connection to the legendary Dracula.

- **12:00 PM:** Indulge in Whitby's culinary heritage by savoring a delicious lunch of fish and chips. Head to one of the many restaurants or cafes along the harbor front, soaking up the lively atmosphere while enjoying the freshest seafood.

Afternoon:

- **1:30 PM:** Take a leisurely stroll along the West Cliff, enjoying stunning views of the coastline and the rugged cliffs. Explore the charming shops selling local crafts and souvenirs, or simply relax on a bench and watch the waves crashing against the shore.

- **3:00 PM:** Step back in time at the Captain Cook Memorial Museum. Delve into the life and voyages of the famous explorer, Captain James Cook, who called Whitby home. Explore a collection of artifacts, maps, and exhibits showcasing his remarkable achievements.

- **4:30 PM:** Enjoy a relaxing afternoon tea at a traditional tea room. Savor a selection of delicate sandwiches, scones with clotted cream and jam, and a pot of freshly brewed tea, immersing yourself in a quintessential English tradition.

Evening:

- **6:00 PM:** As the sun begins to set, take a scenic boat trip along the coastline. Keep your eyes peeled for dolphins, porpoises, or even the occasional whale breaching the surface. Enjoy the breathtaking views of Whitby Abbey bathed in the golden light of dusk.

- **7:30 PM:** Cap off your day with a delicious meal at a local pub. Sample traditional pub fare like steak and ale pie or bangers and mash, paired with a locally brewed cask ale. Soak up the friendly atmosphere and enjoy a relaxing evening.

Weekend Getaway: Whitby and Surrounding Areas

Day One:

- **Morning:** Follow the itinerary for "One Day in Whitby" outlined above, exploring the iconic Whitby Abbey, savoring a delicious fish and chip lunch, and enjoying the stunning views from the West Cliff.

- **Afternoon:** Venture out of Whitby and explore the charming village of Robin Hood's Bay. Explore the maze-like alleyways lined with colorful cottages, descend the steep steps to the pebble beach, and enjoy a refreshing afternoon tea at a quaint cafe.

Day Two:

- **Morning:** Immerse yourself in the beauty of the North York Moors National Park. Embark on a scenic hike through the rolling hills and heather moorland, encountering cascading waterfalls and ancient stone circles. Alternatively, take a journey through time on the North York Moors Railway, a heritage railway offering breathtaking views of the countryside.

- **Afternoon:** Spend the afternoon in the vibrant seaside resort of Scarborough. Stroll along the expansive South Bay Beach, explore the historic Scarborough Castle perched atop a cliff, or experience the thrills and spills at Alpamare water park.

Family-Friendly Activities in Whitby

Whitby offers a plethora of activities to keep families entertained.

- **Morning:** Spend the morning building sandcastles and paddling in the shallow waters of the sandy beach. For the adventurous, try kayaking or stand-up paddleboarding as a family.

- **Afternoon:** Embark on a treasure hunt around Whitby. Create a list of landmarks or hidden gems for your children to find, keeping them engaged and exploring the town in a fun and interactive way.

- **Evening:** Enjoy a family-friendly meal at a pub with a dedicated children's menu. Many pubs offer outdoor seating areas, allowing you to relax and enjoy the evening while your children play in a safe environment. Alternatively, head to the Pantomime at Whitby Pavilion during the festive season. These lively theatrical performances, filled with music, dance, and audience participation, are sure to keep children (and adults!) entertained.

Whitby for History Buffs

Immerse yourself in Whitby's rich and fascinating history with this itinerary:

- **Morning:** Start your day at the Whitby Abbey, delving into its history as a 7th-century monastery and its connection to the legend of Dracula. Afterwards, explore the Captain Cook Memorial Museum, learning about the life and voyages of the famous explorer who called Whitby home.

- **Afternoon:** Visit the Pannett Art Gallery, home to an impressive collection of art and artifacts related to Whitby's maritime history and artistic heritage. Next, take a walk through the historic St. Mary's Church, one of the oldest churches in Whitby, boasting beautiful stained glass windows and a rich history.

- **Evening:** Embark on a Whitby Ghost Tour. Learn about the town's spooky legends and haunted locations, perfect for history buffs with a taste for the macabre. End your evening at a traditional pub, where you can share stories and anecdotes from your day's explorations.

- **Outdoor Adventure Weekend in Whitby**

- Whitby is a paradise for outdoor enthusiasts. This itinerary allows you to experience the best of its natural beauty:

- **Day One:** Embark on a challenging hike along the Cleveland Way National Trail, a 109-mile path offering stunning panoramic views of the North Sea and dramatic cliff formations. Alternatively, explore the rolling hills and hidden valleys of the North York Moors National Park, encountering picturesque villages and ancient monuments.

- **Afternoon:** In the afternoon, try surfing at Sandsend Beach, a short drive from Whitby. Experienced surfers can tackle the challenging waves, while beginners can take lessons and learn the basics. For a different perspective, explore the coastline on a kayak or stand-up paddleboard, enjoying the tranquility of hidden coves and secluded beaches.

- **Day Two:** Spend the morning fishing for cod, mackerel, pollock, or even the occasional sea bass on a chartered boat trip. In the afternoon, tee off at the Royal Whitby Golf Club, a championship course with breathtaking views of the North Sea. Alternatively, enjoy a leisurely round at the scenic Whitby Castle Park Golf Course.

Practical Information

Planning a trip to Whitby ensures an unforgettable experience, but a little preparation goes a long way. Here's a breakdown of essential information to navigate Whitby smoothly and immerse yourself in the local culture.

Safety Tips:

- **Respect the Power of the Sea:** The North Sea can be unpredictable, especially during high tides and strong winds. Always stay a safe distance from the water's edge, particularly on cliff tops and rocky shores. If you plan on venturing out on the water, be sure to check weather conditions beforehand and use reputable boat tour operators.

- **Tide Times Matter:** Whitby's harbor and some coastal areas are significantly affected by tides. Be aware of tide times to avoid getting caught off guard by rising water levels. Local tide tables are readily available online or at tourist information centers.

- **Walking on Uneven Terrain:** Whitby boasts beautiful coastal walks and hikes through the North York Moors National Park. Wear sturdy footwear with good grip, as paths can be uneven and slippery, especially after rain. Be mindful of loose rocks and uneven steps, particularly on cliff walks.

Local Customs and Etiquette:

- **Pub Etiquette:** Pubs are a cornerstone of British social life, and Whitby is no exception. When ordering a drink, approach the bar and wait your turn to be served. It's customary to thank the bartender after receiving your drink. Many pubs allow dogs, but always check with the staff before bringing your furry friend.

- **Respecting Queues:** The British are known for their orderly queuing system. Whether waiting for a table at a restaurant, purchasing tickets, or boarding a bus, politely join the back of the line and avoid cutting in front of others.

- **Cash vs. Card:** While most establishments accept credit and debit cards, carrying some cash is always handy. Smaller shops, cafes, and traditional pubs might not always have card payment facilities.

Useful Phrases:

- **Hello/Goodbye:** Hello, Good morning/afternoon/evening, Goodbye
- **Please/Thank you:** Please, Thank you
- **Excuse me:** Excuse me
- **Do you speak English?:** Do you speak English? (useful if you encounter someone who doesn't speak English fluently)
- **How much is this?:** How much is this?
- **Can I have the bill, please?:** Can I have the bill, please?
- **Cheers! (pronounced "cheeahz"):** Cheers! (a toast used for greetings, thanks, or celebrations)

Emergency Contacts:

- **Emergency Services:** 999 (Dial 999 to reach emergency services for police, ambulance, or fire brigade)

69

- **Whitby Tourist Information Centre:** +44 1947 601 601 (for information on local attractions, events, and transportation)

- **NHS (National Health Service):** 111 (for non-emergency medical advice)

By following these simple tips, you'll be well-equipped to navigate Whitby and have a safe and enjoyable experience. Remember, the locals are friendly and welcoming, so don't hesitate to ask for directions or recommendations. Embrace the opportunity to learn a few basic phrases in English and immerse yourself in the local culture. With a little preparation and a spirit of adventure, your Whitby adventure is sure to be a memorable one.

Conclusion

As the salty breeze whips my hair and the cry of gulls echoes across the harbor, I take a final glance at Whitby Abbey, its imposing ruins silhouetted against the setting sun. This charming coastal town has woven its magic on me. From the exhilarating cliff-top walks to the delicious fish and chips devoured on the harbor front, every moment has been an adventure.

I arrived in Whitby a stranger, drawn by its rich history and captivating beauty. Now, I leave with a backpack full of memories and a heart brimming with gratitude. Whitby surprised me at every turn, from the spooky charm of its ghost stories to the breathtaking landscapes of the North York Moors National Park. I learned to navigate the town's cobbled streets, mastered the art of ordering a pint at a local pub ("Cheers!"), and even braved the bracing North Sea on a kayaking adventure.

But beyond the sights and experiences, Whitby has gifted me something even more valuable – a renewed sense of wonder. Everywhere I turned, there was a story waiting to be discovered. The ancient ruins whispered tales of bygone eras, the rugged coastline spoke of raw power, and the friendly faces of the locals exuded a warmth that made me feel instantly welcome.

As I board the train, ready to embark on the next chapter of my journey, I carry a piece of Whitby with me. It's more than just a collection of photographs or souvenirs; it's a feeling – a sense of adventure, a flicker of curiosity, and a deep appreciation for the beauty and diversity of the world. Whitby wasn't just a destination; it was an experience that has enriched my life in ways I couldn't have predicted.

So, dear reader, if you're seeking an adventure that will leave you breathless, a town that pulses with history and charm, and a place where the locals welcome you with open arms, then look no further than Whitby. Pack your bags, lace up your walking boots, and prepare to be enchanted. Whitby awaits!

Printed in Great Britain
by Amazon